318778

k in to

Wayland 2006

Hamilton
n Manager: Rosamund Saunders
laine Wilkinson

in Great Britain in 2006 by Wayland,
t of Hachette Children's Books

t of Saviour Pirotta to be identified as the author
ork has been asserted by him in the Copyright,
s and Patents Act 1988.

ritish Library Cataloguing in Publication Data
Pirotta, Saviour
We love Divali
1.Divali - Juvenile literature
I. Title
394.2'6545

ISBN 10: 0 7502 48378
ISBN 13: 978-0-7502-4837-2

Printed in China

Wayland
Hachette Children's Books
338 Euston Road, London NW1 3BH

The publishers would like to thank the following for
allowing us to reproduce their pictures in this book:

Alamy: 6, Ark Religion; 8, 12. Fabrice Bettex; 9,
Dinodia Images; 10, Robert Holmes; 13, Paul Gapper;
15, Yograj Jadeja; 16, Paul Doyle; 17, World Religions;
23, David Sanger Photography / aargee stationers: 5 /
Christine Osbourne: 14 / Corbis: 22, Jayanta Shaw, Reuters;
4, Lindsay Hebberd; 19, John Slater; 18, Najlah Feanny /
Thirdangle: cover, 7, 11 / Getty Images: 20, AFP /
Art Directors: 21, Helene Rogers.

We Love
DIVALI

Saviour Pirotta

© copyright W

Editor: Kirst
Senior Desi
Designer: F

Published
an imprin

The righ
of the v
Design

All rig
UK
stor
prio
of
li

WAYLAND

Contents

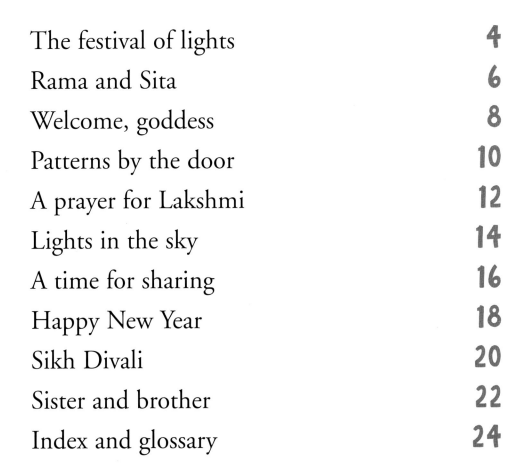

The festival of lights

Welcome to Divali, the festival of light and happiness. It's time to clean your house. It's time to buy new clothes and stock up on sweets. And don't forget to send Divali cards to your friends.

These people are decorating their house for Divali.

4

Divali takes place over five days in October and November. It is the biggest festival of the Hindu year. Sikhs and **Jains** celebrate Divali too.

Divali cards tell your friends you are thinking of them.

DID YOU KNOW?

Divali takes place in the Hindu months of Ashwin and Kartik.

Rama and Sita

During Divali, people from northern India celebrate the return of King Rama and his bride, Princess Sita, to their kingdom. Rama's followers lit thousands of lamps to show Rama and Sita the way.

The demon king **Ravana** had kidnapped Sita. In this picture Rama is fighting him to save her.

These children have lit Divali lamps to show that light wins over darkness.

Today, people still light lamps or candles at Divali to remember the holy king and his princess bride.

DID YOU KNOW?

Monkeys also helped Rama and Sita to escape from Ravana.

Welcome, goddess

Some houses in England are lit up for Divali.

Divali lights are also lit to invite the goddess **Lakshmi** into people's homes. Lakshmi is the goddess of wealth. A visit from her means good luck for the whole year.

HAPPY DIVALI

Colourful paper lanterns light up the streets.

Lamps and candles are placed in windows, outside houses and on roofs. Even shops, offices, garages and streets are decorated with Divali lamps. People know that Lakshmi will visit the houses with the brightest lights.

Patterns by the door

To welcome Lakshmi and visitors, children help to draw **Rangoli** patterns by their front door. Most Rangoli patterns are made of coloured sand or rice powder mixed with water.

The white paste used to make these patterns stands for **purity**.

They include pictures of birds, flowers, stars, moons and gods. Many draw pictures of tiny footsteps too. These show that Lakshmi has visited the house.

These children are drawing Rangoli patterns with coloured paints.

A prayer for Lakshmi

This statue of Lakshmi has been decorated with flowers.

People set up a special **altar** for Lakshmi in their homes. They decorate it with flowers, lights and sometimes coins. Children sing special songs at the altar.

The grown-ups pray that Lakshmi will bring them luck in the coming year. All through the festival people leave their windows open so that Lakshmi can come into their house.

People buy **garlands** of flowers from the market to place at their altars.

Lights in the sky

Divali is the day of light. The burning lamps remind people to thank the gods for all they have. Everyone celebrates good winning over evil and light winning over darkness.

Children have fun with sparklers on Divali night.

Sparklers and firecrackers are let off.
In many cities there are huge
firework displays.

In some
countries Divali
fireworks go on
for many
nights.

DID YOU KNOW?

The noisy fireworks remind the
gods that the people are happy
and thankful.

A time for sharing

These Divali sweets are made with milk, nuts and spices.

Divali is a time for sharing good food. People spend days preparing sweets and snacks to eat with their friends and family. Round and square sweets decorated with nuts and raisins are very popular.

Children also have a special Divali porridge with rice or **sago**. Divali dinner is often a vegetarian curry. The different vegetables in it remind people of a good **harvest**.

Everyone brings food to the **temple** altar for the gods and for each other.

Happy New Year

The day after Divali is New Year's Day. It is a time of new beginnings. Everyone wears new clothes. Families visit friends and relatives and exchange presents. Children touch the feet of grown up relatives to get blessings and money.

Families and friends get together and enjoy the celebrations.

People buy new things for their houses. It's lucky to spend some money on New Year's Day.

Buying cooking pots is especially lucky on New Year's Day.

DID YOU KNOW?

People pay back money they have borrowed, enemies make up and farmers sow new crops.

Sikh Divali

For Sikhs, Divali is a double celebration. The first stone of the Golden Temple in Amritsar, the holy Sikh city, was laid on Divali many years ago.

Many people come to see the Golden Temple lit up for Divali.

It was also on Divali that a Sikh leader, Guru Hargobind Sahib, was released from prison. His followers covered the Golden Temple with lights to welcome him back. Ever since, Sikhs have celebrated Divali in his honour.

Guru Hargobind Sahib was a famous Sikh leader.

21

Sister and brother

The last day of the Divali festival is a special day for brothers and sisters. Sisters cook their brothers' favourite dishes. They place a red dot, a tilak, on their brothers' forehead.

Bengali women pray for their brothers on the last day of Divali.

In return, their brothers give them nice presents. They bless them too. It's a wonderful end to the festival of light and joy. Everyone looks forward to Divali again next year.

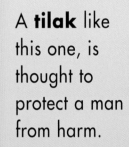

A **tilak** like this one, is thought to protect a man from harm.

Index and glossary

altar a surface used for making offerings to a god or goddess

garlands wreaths of flowers worn or hung up for decoration

harvest the gathering of crops

Jain someone who believes in Jainism, an Indian religion

Lakshmi the Hindu goddess of wealth

purity pureness and cleanliness

rangoli sacred patterns that are painted outside houses and temples

Ravana the many-headed demon king from the Hindu Ramayana

sago the powdered pith of the sago plum, used in puddings

temple a building used for the worship of a god or gods

tilak a dot placed on the forehead, thought to protect men from harm